MW01138535

When Cancer Interrupts

···

David Powlison

New
Growth
Press

WWW.NEWGROWTHPRESS.COM

New Growth Press, Greensboro, NC 27404
www.newgrowthpress.com
Copyright © 2015 by David Powlison

Cover Design: Faceout Books, faceoutstudio.com
Typesetting: Lisa Parnell, lparnell.com

ISBN: 978-1-942572-26-8 (Print)
ISBN: 978-1-942572-27-5 (eBook)

Library of Congress Cataloging-in-Publication Data
Powlison, David, 1949–
  When cancer interrupts / David Powlison.
    pages cm
  ISBN 978-1-942572-26-8 (print) —
  ISBN 978-1-942572-27-5 (ebook)
1. Cancer—Patients—Religious life. I. Title.
  BV4910.33.P67 2015
  248.8'6196994—dc23

                                                    2015003651

Printed in Canada

22 21 20 19 18 17 16 15   1 2 3 4 5

Some surprises in life are wonderful—a long-hoped-for pregnancy, a windfall inheritance, an unexpected promotion. But a cancer diagnosis is *never* a good surprise. When the doctor says "It's cancer," those words break into your life in a most unpleasant, threatening way. You feel violated. The enemy is operating on the inside—is part of you. It is a bit like coming home after an evening out to discover your home broken into, every drawer ransacked, and your most treasured possession stolen. You feel betrayed. The enemy got inside.

My life has been interrupted on four occasions by a cancer diagnosis. And, of course, the diagnosis is just the beginning. It is rapidly followed by tests, surgeries, pain, the healing process, chemo, and the ongoing follow-up. My particular cancer and recovery was different each time. But every time triggered an honest inner struggle. What if . . . ? What about the people I love? What is my life? What will my future hold? Do I in fact trust the God in whom I say I believe? Those are the big, life-defining questions. And there are little struggles too, because cancer drastically alters the usual pattern of life. What things must I do tomorrow that I never planned to do? Threatening surprises change your life instantly and obviously. That threat can leave you disoriented, overwhelmed, and anxious.

When cancer blindsides you, your mind usually spins with questions and uncertainties. But in the midst of the turmoil, there is a place to turn. You can go to someone for immediate help.

> God is our refuge and strength,
> a very present help in trouble.
> Therefore we will not fear though the earth
>   gives way. (Psalm 46:1–2)

Those are not just words in a book. When you take them to heart, you find them true. Those who actually ask receive. Those who seek do find. Those who knock find the door wide open.

O Lord, you are my refuge. Protect me. You are my strength. Strengthen me. You promise to be a very present help in my trouble. This is trouble. Help.

And he does. No one wants to hear the words "You have cancer." But as you learn how Christ takes the fear away, you are receiving a wonderful gift that you will treasure for the rest of your life. Christians who learn to suffer well often say something along these lines: "I would never choose to go through what I had to go through. But I would not give up what I learned in the process. God met me. My faith became real."

We will look at four steps in how we come to grips with a cancer diagnosis. Take your time. Listen. Learn to walk through the experience in the right way.

What You Are Experiencing Matters

First, you can be honest about how hard it is. You don't have to live in denial. You don't have to live as if you can beat this by willpower and medical intervention. God is up to something far more significant. Reflect on what the apostle Peter says to people who face serious threats. He points out that they are being "grieved by various trials" (1 Peter 1:6). He recognizes the difficult road they had to walk. He doesn't sugarcoat it. He doesn't say "You can do it." He doesn't say "Just keep busy or take something so you don't have to think about it. Instead, he invites you to get personal. Why does he say "*various* trials"? He is giving you a blank check that you can fill in with your particular details. The Bible puts things in a way that draws you in. God invites you to name exactly what you are facing.

A bit later in his letter Peter describes these trials as "fiery" (4:12). In other words, this is dangerous; it burns, it hurts, you might die. That is a good description of cancer. It brings pain physically, emotionally, and spiritually. It tests you—and that is exactly where Christ meets you.

God always invites his people to *name* their particular troubles. You can be like the writers of the Psalms and tell him all about what you are facing, feeling, and thinking. Below is a list of the kinds of things that people experience when cancer interrupts. Check the ones that apply to you. At the end of the list is space for you to describe any particular troubles that I haven't mentioned.

1. *Uncertainty.* One of the hardest parts of any trial is that you do not know how things will turn out. The outcome of cancer is uncertain. An experienced doctor will talk with you about percentages. He may predict a likely trajectory and can offer both realism and a degree of comfort by what he has seen in similar cases. Online research will usually supplement your knowledge about what you are facing. Still, cancer is a wild card. Because it threatens your life from the inside, percentages and statistics only take you so far. Good odds for survival are not the only thing we'd like to know. We'd also like to know what the process will be like. We'd like to be one hundred percent sure of our survival. And we can't be that certain.

2. *Pain.* You don't know what will happen, but you do know it will hurt. Depending on your diagnosis, you could be facing a whole host of painful experiences—invasive tests, surgery, a hospital stay, chemotherapy, and so forth. For all the wonderful skills and advances in modern medicine, you can't avoid experiencing some "discomfort," to use the word the doctors use. I call it pain! And physical pain is often

accompanied by the pain of being in a dehumanizing environment. The beeping noises, the equipment, that stylish hospital gown, the institutional décor, the nurse fixated on writing notes rather than looking at you. It is a "fiery" trial at many levels.

3. *Fears.* The natural human responses to pain and uncertainty are fear and anxiety. You are in uncharted territory. Much of what is happening or might happen triggers the inward stress of responding to threat. Our natural wiring can easily run out of control into worry, fretting, brooding, and even an anxiety attack.

4. *Questions.* A life-changing diagnosis raises so many questions. What will happen? Will I make it? What will I be able to do? How will my family handle it? Does my insurance cover it? What if I can't _____ (go to work, function as a parent, have sex, go to the bathroom normally, get out of bed)? Is God punishing me? Why did this happen? Do people care?

5. *Loss.* Those questions inevitably have to do with loss. The natural human response to loss is sorrow. What will you lose? How will you handle those losses? Of course you are concerned with your health, but then there are all those things you are able to do when healthy that you might not be able to do as you go through cancer treatments. And of course the

final loss—death—is one possibility with many cancer diagnoses. Sorrow can deepen and then freeze into depression.

6. *Blame.* When something goes wrong, one natural human response is to assign blame. A cancer diagnosis always interrupts whatever you were doing and frustrates whatever plans you had. Do you get angry? Anger can point in many directions. Some people wallow in self-recrimination and regrets. Others blame the doctor. Or take it out on family members. Or accuse God. Cancer is never "in my plans"—so who messed up what was supposed to happen?

7. *Becoming your diagnosis.* Of course the people who love you are very concerned about your cancer. But it's easy for people to forget that you are not just a diagnosis. When that happens, even your loved ones tend to only ask about your health, how you are coming along, or your prognosis. Medical personnel are always tempted to view patients as "the kidney cancer in room 218." But there is so much more to you. There is what you did that day, what you are thinking about, who you talked with, and what your emotional and spiritual struggles are. There is always a person inside the cancer diagnosis, but people rarely ask "How are *you* doing?" In the middle of a health crisis, the person you actually are can be overlooked by those around you.

8. *Unhelpful advice.* Of course the people around you are very concerned about your health. But one entire book of the Bible is a cautionary tale about how people respond poorly to the affliction of others. In the Bible, Job's three friends significantly compound his affliction by their questions and advice. Our contemporary culture is so obsessed with finding explanations and cures that people's way of coming at you can make you feel as if you are being blamed for your cancer. What foods have you been eating? Were you exercising regularly? Shouldn't you be a vegetarian? Are you a smoker? Have you been allowing stress to jack up your cortisol levels? Many people are quick to offer you a book, tell you what worked for them, or give you a pep talk. Of course no one intends to blame, but the line of questioning and the implicit or explicit advice steadily identifies you as the responsible party. Meanwhile, you are still facing cancer.

9. *Any other particular struggles?*

_____

_____

_____

_____

_____

_____

Cancer is a fiery trial. And it is helpful to name what is hard. But what do you do next?

Remember That God Himself Is with You

You may go to the one who loves you. You may bring your struggles and tell him all about them. Remember who he is. He cares. He is involved. He is a sure and certain presence. He will walk with you through pain. He will strengthen you and give you courage. He will deliver you from your fears. He is your refuge, a safe place amid danger. He will clarify your thinking. He will anchor your hopes in what can never be lost. He is merciful to you, and he will make you merciful. He will settle you in your true identity. He will advise you about things far more important than cancer. Take the list in the previous section and cry out your troubles to the God who hears and who promises to never leave you or forsake you (Psalm 28:6; Hebrews 13:5). Who God *is* speaks to every problem on the list.

Cancer is always a test of faith. And cancer always creates an opportunity for faith to grow. Faith is nourished on who God says he is. He is what he says. Faith feeds on who God promises to be. He says what he does, and does what he says. Remember. Take him at his word.

Many biblical truths will serve and bless you in your struggle, but the simple reality that "God is with you" overarches all. It is a summary of all God's blessings to you. The promise of God's caring, committed, merciful presence through *all* of life in *every* circumstance is a primary strand of biblical DNA. This reality weaves through all of Scripture. It is woven into the life of every one of God's children. Again and again God repeats to his people "I will never leave you." In all kinds of ways, in all kinds of circumstances, "I will never forsake you." He reminds us, "Though you walk through the valley of the shadow of death I will be with you. Though the mountains fall into the sea I will be with you. I will not leave you as an orphan. I will come to you" (Psalms 23:4; 46:2; John 14:18).

Cancer is not an exception to the rule. It is where the rule comes true.

It is easy to forget that God is an actual person. We so easily forget. That is why he so often reminds us: Remember! He takes the initiative. He willingly comes to you. He is not an idea, an energy, an experience you work up within yourself. We hear his words to us in the Bible, revealing how Jesus embodies the Yes! to all his promises and purposes. But he is not bound within the pages of the book. His book reveals the one who speaks, who is I AM. He is active. He walks with us. He tells us his names so we can talk with him. He is your hands-on Father. He is the Vinedresser at work pruning you to make you fruitful. He is your good Shepherd who gave his life for his sheep. He walks with you and watches over you. He is the Holy Spirit who makes his home in you so that you become a person of faith and love. This most wondrous Person is the game changer. He is for you in this very moment as you deal with cancer.

It is a great good when family, friends, and medical personnel walk alongside you during your struggles in life. It is an even greater good to know that God is with you. No mere human can understand exactly what you are going through, can get on the inside, can rewrite the script of your heart. Each of the many times I have gone under anesthesia, I have realized that I am alone in some essential way. No one else is going through this experience. I will be put to sleep. I will be completely helpless. When I awake, I will be in pain (unless this is the time when I awake in God's presence and see him face-to-face). Each time, by God's grace, and by my intention, I have fallen asleep with Psalm 23 filling my mind. As I drift off, I walk through different parts of the psalm. The Lord is my shepherd. He restores my soul. He is with me. His goodness and mercy follow closely after me. I will live in his home forever.

God's Word speaks of who he actually is. Cancer is my true enemy, one of the many shadows of death, one of the many evils. But Christ willingly walks with me through every valley shadowed by death. He is willingly your Shepherd too. Remember. It takes looking to him in the neediness and dependency of faith. Ask and you will receive. Ask for mercy for all the ways you do not follow him. Trust his death in your place, the price for all of your wrongs. This cancer might mean death. I hope not. You hope not. But it is certainly a shadow of what will come sooner or later. And our good Shepherd bore death for you. He walked through the valley so that we will become free from the fear of death. If you seek him, you will find him. Cling to him by faith, and you can be certain that you, like him, will live forever.

That introduces our third step. We have named our troubles. We have remembered the one who entered our troubles to save us from our troubles. Now we cling to him.

Cling to Christ

The Lord describes our relationship with him from many perspectives. Love him. Fear him. Walk in his ways. Entrust yourself to him. Believe his promises. Seek him. Do what he says. Serve him. Yet he knows that we tend to get stuck in ruts—I do anyway, and I'm pretty sure you do too. So he keeps coming at us from different directions. Here is one way the Bible puts it that we don't often hear mentioned: *cling* to him. Hold on tight. Be glued to him. Don't let him go. Hold fast.

What does it mean to cling to Christ by faith when you face a threatening cancer diagnosis? Faith has two core activities: dire need, then utter joy. The order matters. First, we are weak and need his help. Second, knowing his care, we become strong and joyful. When cancer intrudes into your body and changes your life, you are invited to become aware of your dire need for help. Many psalms cry out to God in need. We cling to Christ. We ask the Lord to save us from our real troubles, real sins, real sufferings, and real anguish. When cancer interrupts, your faith must come to life. This hard thing, cancer, leads to a great mercy.

If your faith does not come to life in your weakness and need, then fear and false hopes take over. "I'm deathly afraid" and "I can beat this" are evil twins. On the one hand, fear bullies you into putting your ultimate hope in something that's never good enough—doctors, percentages, treatments, a cure, strategies for self-healing, keeping yourself busy, self-numbing. On the other hand, pride and self-trust seduce you into thinking that you don't need to be afraid, that faith is a crutch for weak people, and that you can be stronger than cancer and stronger than the shadow of death.

When you instead take your struggles to God, you find that he *is* with you. Even if death should happen to win this skirmish, life wins the great war.

You don't need to fear the "what-ifs." Because Christ triumphed over literal death, you will live. Joy, courage, and loving purpose get the last say. Cling to him, because he is your refuge and your strength. Cling to him. He is a very present help in trouble. He gives strength when you are weak. He is merciful when you are barely holding it together. When your reactions to suffering take you in a wrong direction, you can turn back to him because he is still merciful. Every part of who God is in redeeming love speaks into your sufferings and says, "Cling to me."

Amazingly, along with deep and dire need, you will then also find utter joy. God is reliable, and faith that relies now sings in gladness, gratitude, and celebration. The psalmists who cry their grief to God then cry out their gladness and adoration—often in the same psalm. In one word, "Hallelujah!" In a few sentences,

> Bless the Lord, O my soul,
> and let everything in me bless his holy
>   name!
> Bless the Lord, O my soul,
> and do not forget any of the good things
>   he does!
>   —paraphrase of Psalm 103:1–2

I never wanted to have cancer. No one does. But by going through hard times, my faith grows up.

Cancer is meant to get us to look death in the eye. Faith deepens as need deepens. So joy deepens. We become less childish in how we believe. Psalm 90:12 says, "Teach us to number our days that we may get a heart of wisdom." Facing cancer the right way, we become true grown-ups—which is to say we become more childlike. We learn to simply need our Father and the mercies of his only-begotten Son. And we learn to simply delight in him.

Finally, the fourth step follows.

Faith Moves into Love for Others

Faith always expresses itself in practical love for other people. As you go to God and express your need and your joy, your faith will branch out into loving concern for the people in your life (Galatians 5:6). Cancer is one of the defining killers in our era. It is a typical struggle. Only a few generations ago infectious diseases were the great threat. Most people did not live long enough to get cancer, and if they did get cancer they did not survive to have four kinds of cancer. As you learn to face your cancer, you are growing in wisdom to help others who also face a typical struggle.

Loving others may seem like an insurmountable wall to climb when you are in the midst of your own struggle physically, emotionally, and spiritually. But you will start to love even in the way you struggle. For example, loving those around you in the midst of your weakness can be as simple as sharing your weakness and need with someone else. Men sometimes have a harder time than women being honest about weakness and expressing it to others. But unloving reticence, the pretense of having it together, is not just a male tendency. The truth is that most people don't really like needing help. The Bible is candid about our weakness. David wrote many psalms out of his sense of weakness and need. Jesus asked his disciples to watch and pray with him in his dire need. Paul often shared his personal need with the church—pressures that almost overwhelmed him, his thorn in his flesh, and the sorrows God had spared him (2 Corinthians 4:8; 12:7; Philippians 2:27).

A healthy candor will revitalize relationships as you get personal and open your heart to others. Don't simply speak about your physical condition. Be candid about how you are doing as a person. Let others in on your sorrows, apprehensions, and joys. Speak about what you are learning in relationship to Christ. Share where you are struggling, and where you aspire to grow. Beyond asking people to pray for physical healing, you can say "Pray for me that I will know God's presence when my courage fails me and I'm afraid." Or "Pray for me that I won't be irritable when I'm feeling sick from chemotherapy."

Every cancer raises spiritual issues, so talk about them. Asking for prayer beyond your physical needs opens up the door for conversations about the most important things in life. Cancer creates opportunities for more profound intimacy with those around you. People pay attention when a sufferer is being honest.

Here is another simple way that you can love even in the midst of the turmoil of cancer diagnosis and treatment. Learn the names of those who are caring for you. This has become very significant for me. It is a litmus test for my heart. Am I so self-preoccupied that I do not notice the people caring for me? Or is trust in the Lord actually working out into remembering names, into humor, into being observant, into saying thank you? Medical people have a hard job. In this case, their job is to care for me well! They earn a living by showing practical love. Not only is the work hard, it can be thankless. Fearful, grouchy, self-absorbed patients don't say thank you. To recognize what someone does for you is a way of loving them back. It humanizes a medical experience that can be dehumanizing for all of us. Medical personnel often suffer from compassion fatigue. Simple forms of caring about them communicate our shared humanity amid this difficult, sometimes squalid, and always painful experience.

Other aspects of love will unfold over time. Paul tells us that the comfort each one of us receives in our particular afflictions overflows to others, whatever they are facing (2 Corinthians 1:3–11). By God's grace, my cancers have not been mortal. Though the treatments I have gone through have often been hard, I have learned some things that can help others who may be facing even more serious threats. My willingness to enter the experience of vulnerability and pain teaches empathy for others who face hard things. I have a feel for what someone else is going through. My experience also teaches sympathy. I know how hard it is, so I care, and want to help if I can. Learning how to walk through a cancer diagnosis in faith gives me something good to give away to others. Just like me, other people need to learn candor with God and to remember his mercies, how to seek and find him, and how faith might translate into love. Cancer immerses you in the valley of the shadow of death. All the ways you grow as you walk through that experience can be given away and become useful to other people.

A Closing Word

No two human beings have exactly the same experience of cancer. No two of us work through trouble in exactly the same way. I have sought to describe in four simple steps what gets worked out in a profoundly personal process.

- Be candid about your trouble.
- Remember who God is.
- Cling to Christ.
- Let faith move into love for others.

What this will look like in your life is your unique story to tell.

One of the beauties of biblical truth is that the same themes play out in all of us, yet each one of us brings a unique story line. The last line of the Gospel of John is one of my favorite sentences because it demonstrates how this is so. Consider what John has been doing for twenty-one chapters. He has written Jesus's story by telling about different people who met Jesus. John closes by saying, "Now there are also many other things that Jesus did. Were every one of them to be written, I suppose that the world itself could not contain the books that would be written" (John 21:25). Every story about what Jesus did, does, and will do has a similar theme. And yet each person's story is different, and the differences matter. God writes down all the stories. Your version of the story—how Jesus's mercy works out in your life—matters.

When the words "You have cancer" interrupt your life, it always raises a spiritual challenge.

Suffering is meant to lead you to God and strengthen your faith in Christ our Savior. It is meant to wean you away from self-absorption, unbelief, false beliefs, and sins.

If God has not yet befriended you and become your ever-present help in trouble, if you have not yet sought him and relied on his mercies, then a cancer diagnosis will magnify your problems. You may become bitter, despairing, addictive, fearful, or frenzied. Even if you "beat" this cancer on this occasion, it may only make you more foolishly self-confident, more fixated on a medical salvation, and more invested in avoiding the God to whom you are accountable. If you have been on the run from the one who actually beat death once and for all, then stop. Turn around. Seek his mercy. He is mercy incarnate, and his door stands wide open.

If you are God's child, if you belong to him, then a cancer diagnosis—in Christ's hands—will change you for the good. He will teach you the things we have been talking about. Sometimes he will change you quickly; always he will change you slowly. The Lord is simultaneously urgent and patient. He calls you to trust him right now. He's urgent, so act on what you've read. He is pleased to work in you over your lifetime. He's patient, so don't despair at the fact that you still struggle. By his grace, over time, you will come to terms with life and death on his terms. He will gentle you, purify you, cleanse you of your self-absorption. He will make you need him and love him. He will rearrange your priorities so that first things come first more often. He will walk with you.

Of course you will fail at times. You may be seized by irritability, brooding, escapism, or fear. You may flounder. But he will always pick you up when you stumble. With him, for Jesus's sake, there is always forgiveness (1 John 1:9–10). Continue seeking and finding your Savior. Your inner enemy, that moral cancer 10,000 times more deadly than any physical cancer, will be dying, and you will be walking in the path of life.

> Out of the depths I cry to you, O Lord!
> O Lord, hear my voice! Let your ears
> be attentive to the voice of my pleas for
> mercy! If you, O Lord, should mark iniq-
> uities, O Lord, who could stand? But with
> you there is forgiveness, that you may be
> feared. (Psalm 130:1–4)

Because of Christ, we are forgiven. Because of Christ, we stand. Because of Christ, we hope. With Christ, even though we die, we live forever.

> *Though I walk through the valley of the shadow of death, I will fear no evil. Bless the Lord, O my soul.*

Simple, Quick, Biblical

Advice on Complicated Counseling Issues
for Pastors, Counselors, and Individuals

MINIBOOK
CATEGORIES

- Personal Change
- Marriage & Parenting
- Medical & Psychiatric Issues
- Women's Issues
- Singles
- Military

USE YOURSELF | GIVE TO A FRIEND | DISPLAY IN YOUR CHURCH OR MINISTRY

New
Growth
Press

Go to **www.newgrowthpress.com** or call **336.378.7775** to
purchase individual minibooks or the entire collection.
Durable acrylic display stands are also available to house
the minibook collection.